Video Marketing Pro

Professional Video Marketing Strategies to Boost Leads, Sales and ROI

Chris King

Table of Contents

Introduction

Best Places to Use Video

4 Steps to Creating a Great Video Campaign

Creating Videos

   Video Equipment *(For All Types of Videos)*

   6 Types of Viral Videos

   More Great Ideas to Make Videos About

   How to Make Your Video Stand Out From Your Competitors

Top 7 Video Distribution Sites

3 Keys to Success with Video Marketing

Video Marketing Metrics *(What You Should Be Tracking)*

BONUS: YouTube SEO for #1 Google Rankings (Checklist)

Conclusion

Bonus:

Free Video Reveals _How to Get_

$1,000, $3,000 & $5,000 Commissions

Deposited Directly Into Your Bank

Account without Every Picking up the

Phone

Watch Now - > **http://bit.ly/1k-3k-5k**

Disclaimer

This book has been written for information purposes only. Every effort has been made to make this book as complete and accurate as possible. However, there may be mistakes in typography or content. Also, this book provides information only up to the publishing date. Therefore, this book should be used as a guide - not as the ultimate source.

The purpose of this book is to educate. The author and the publisher does not warrant that the information contained in this book is fully complete and shall not be responsible for any errors or omissions. The author and publisher shall have neither liability nor responsibility to any person or entity with respect to any loss or damage caused or alleged to be caused directly or indirectly by this book.

Introduction

Online video has burst onto the scene as arguably the best promotion strategy for both large and small business alike!

Whatever your business is, video gives you more opportunities to expand your brand and share you message with the world at a very affordable cost.

Here are a couple of highlights of why you should be using video marketing in everything you do:

1.	YouTube is the second most popular search engine, right after Google, which of course owns YouTube.
2.	YouTube alone gets more than 4 billion views per day (Plus there are more great

places to upload video we'll talk about later)

3.   Online video accounts for more than 50% of all mobile traffic (if you're not optimizing for mobile you're missing at least 50% of your potential traffic)

On top of all that video is also:

- Low cost: as previously mentioned, online videos require very little investment to create. Essentially what you need are a web-cam and a YouTube account.

- Video allows you to connect on a more personal level with your audience. People are much more likely to trust you and relate to you when they can see you and hear your voice.

- It's great for your search engine rankings: Google loves to place video on page #1 because it loves to give searchers a variety of media. Most people don't take the time to create these videos. This gives you a huge leg up on the competition!

-Video is easy to share: About 700 YouTube videos are shared every minute on Twitter alone! Just imagine Facebook, Instagram, Pinterest and others. When you combine them you're talking about 1,000's of shares per minute!

-Video levels the playing field: Lets face it...not every business can afford television advertising. But I'm going to show you a way in this book you can get television quality advertising for pennies on the dollar. Plus, it will be more targeted than television.

-Gives you quick feedback: Let's say you shoot a video and post it on your Facebook page...how long would it take to get feedback from your fans? Not very long right? You can easily test different videos and get feedback before using them in any type of ad campaign.

Best Places to Use Video

Let's quickly go over some places you should be using video in your business:

1. On you website: The home page of your website needs a welcome video. We're in a video age. People want to watch a video about your business instead of reading text.

2. On your blog: It's always a good idea to give your clients multiple ways of viewing the information you are sharing. So if you have an article on your blog you could easily share some additional tips surrounding that topic by creating a video to go along with it.

3. Social Media: There's not way around it social media loves pictures and video. Micro videos (short 15 sec. or less video) are now becoming very popular as well.

4. Product demonstration: Just think about how much product gets sold on infomercials every day. Product demonstrations work! So make sure you are suing them.

5. Client testimonials: There's nothing more powerful than testimonials. I would suggest having a mix of video testimonials and text testimonials.

6. Tutorials: These are important for when consumers need step by step instructions on how to use specific products and services.

4 Steps to Creating a Great Video Campaign

The entire process of creating quality online video boils down to four steps:

1. Setting the goals for you video
2. Creating a compelling message
3. Deciding what format to shoot the video
4. Distribution and promoting your video

Step #1: Goals

What is your goal with the video you are shooting? You need to decide this up front. Here are a few ideas:

1.   Building your brand
2.   Getting website traffic
3.   Building credibility and trust
4.   Creating a sale
5.   Etc...

Deciding this ahead of time will help you create a compelling call to action. In my opinion you have to start with knowing the call to action...because ultimately that's what it's all about...getting the customer to take some sort of action that benefits your business.

Step #2: Message

What's the overall message you are trying to get across? You don't have very much time to capture your audience's attention so I always like to have at least 3 things planned out ahead of time:

1. Strong opening line – Get their attention right out of the gate
2. Content – Whatever you are shooting a video about
3. Call to action – Make sure to have a strong call to action. At least have a call to action at the end…if not you can put one through the video.

Step #3: Video Format:

There are several great ways to record video. So if you're someone who just trembles at the idea of getting in front of a camera...don't worry:

1. Webcam: this is probably the fastest and simplest option
2. Webinar: you can always record your webinars and host the replay
3. Traditional video: Using tripod and video camera
4. Screen capture: You can easily record a powerpoint video with programs like camtasia, jingproject or screenflow
5. Video montage: there a several tools like Animoto.com that allow you to import photos and text to create a video.

Depending on the overall goal of the video will help you determine which of these methods is the best. Ill cover more of the equipment I use in the next chapter called "Choosing the Right Video Equipment".

Step #4: Distribution:

YouTube is usually the first place people think of uploading their video and it makes sense because they are the biggest. You would be missing on a potentially thousands of visitors if you didn't take advantage of all of the other free platforms as well. I'll give you a full breakdown on those in the chapter called "Top 7 Distribution Sites" and "Paid Platforms"

Creating Videos

Video Equipment *(For All Types of Videos)*

Many people think that you need to spend thousands of dollars to get a high quality video and that is just not the case. With today's smart phones you can actually shoot most video very cheaply and easily using just your phone.

But just in case you want to step it up a notch or you want to shoot other types of video let me give you some of the resources I use.

Webinar recordings: There are several platforms that offer webinar recording but the one I suggest is http://gotomeeting.com

Traditional Video:

-Video camera: you can use anything from your iPhone on up to a $2,000 camera. Personally I use the iPhone unless Im paying a professional photographer.

-Tripod: Whatever camera you choose having a good tripod is a must. You don't want shaky videos.

-Lighting Kit: I use a "Cowboy Studio 2275. You can find this kit on Amazon for about $200. But any 3 point lighting kit will work.

-Lavalier microphone: This is a microphone that will clip right onto your shirt so you get a nice crisp sound even though you'll be a distance away from the camera.

Screen Recordings:

-Camtasia: Great for high quality videos that you will be hosting on on a platform like Vimeo. You can download a free trial at

http://www.techsmith.com/camtasia.html

-Jing: This is great if you are shooting videos that are under 5 minutes. Jing videos can be hosted free on screencast.com – you can download Jing for free at http://www.techsmith.com/jing.html

-Screenflow: like Camtasia but it's for Mac users. It's also a little bit cheaper at $99. You can download it here:

http://www.telestream.net/screenflow/overview.htm

-Blue Yeti Microphone: This is the gold standard of microphones. If you shooting screen recordings you absolutely need one. Find out more here: http://www.bluemic.com/yeti/

Video Montage:
- http://Animoto.com

Other:

-Video Scribe: Have you ever seen those videos where someone is drawing on the screen while someone is talking? That is what Video Scribe does. If you were to have someone do the drawing for you it would cost thousands of dollars but Video Scribe has a service for $13.50 per month that allows you do your own. You can find our more at http://VideoScribe.co

6 Types of Viral Videos

Everyone always ask "how do I get my video to go viral?" and it's a great question because it can get a lot of traffic however it isn't something I would suggest aiming all of your efforts at. Focus on creating value and if you have an opportunity to work in some of these elements to you video then take it!

1. Emotional Response

Find out if your video elicits a strong emotional response. When a video elicits strong emotions it creates a strong urge to share. There are many types of connection you can make in your videos including:

- Children
- Money
- Religion
- Race
- Family
- Greed
- Humor
- Illness
- And more...

Just focus on making a connection with at least 1 emotional response

2. Children and Animals (Cute things)

Humans are wired to gawk at cuteness. Have you ever seen the YouTube video about the cat jumping in all the boxes? These videos go viral in a hurry! Just look up "Maru" the cat on YouTube to see what I mean. People love cute animals doing all sorts of things.

Children are another way to get your video to go viral fast. If you look up "funny babies" on YouTube right now you'll see all the top videos have at least 1,000,000 views or more!

So just think about how you can incorporate cute little things in your videos.

3. Newsworthy content

Seemingly anything these world leaders do or say is newsworthy! Because the political parties are so divided the entire media just fuels the outrage. No matter what kind of political video you put up is going to have lovers and haters! This fuels emotions like anger, outrage and disgust; and these types of videos spread virally. That can very good for getting comments on your content.

But it doesn't just have to be political news. Any kind of news is great for sharing on video. Just flip through any newspaper or magazine to find great ideas for your videos.

4. Humor

Who doesn't love a good laugh? Everyone does! Even before YouTube "Americas Funniest Home Videos" was capitalizing on this. Some time ago, when I first got started in online marketing, I started a blog that all I did was put funny videos on it and share the blog posts. Each video had an ad for an affiliate product on the side bar or down below it. Believe it or not that blog was shared hundreds of times per day and turned a nice profit! The takeaway for me was...people love funny stuff!

5. Shocking

Shock and awe! Think of the last video you saw that shocked you...did you want to share it with someone? Most people do. That's what were going for here. Some of the most viral videos with shock factor really push the boundaries on what is right and wrong to share on video but that's what creates the shock factor. So don't be afraid to push the envelope!

6. Parody

Dozens of brands have parodied popular videos for their own agenda and in some cases, they experience great success. Nearly every musical artist has some sort of parody on YouTube. All you have to do is think about how you can work your message into a parody.

More Great Ideas to Make Videos About

Here are some more ideas to kick start your creative thinking on what to shoot videos on.

- Testimonials

- Answer common questions.

- Overcome objections

- Add subtitles for hearing impaired

- Inspirational video

- Tell stories that relate to your product

- Get a local celebrity to film a video for you

- Add professional voiceovers

- Teach something

- Behind the scenes video footage

- Introduce your team

- Piggyback on a current event

- Publicity stunts

- Personal stories

- Random thoughts

- Time lapse videos

- Controversial statements

- Pose a question, or puzzle

- Review videos

- Don't_____ before you watch this video

- Public poll video

- Issue a challenge

- Cover a large event.

- Show them what your typical day is like.

- Hidden camera videos

Of course there are many more video ideas but this should help you get started!

How to Make Your Video Stand Out From Your Competitors

Plan your script ahead of time

When I say plan your "script" what I actually mean is your video "outline". You want to be confident in what you are saying with you video but at the same time you don't want to be reading. So generally what I do is plan 3 big areas ahead of time.. So it would look like this

- Intro
- Content (use bullet points to lay out what you're going to say)
- Call to action

Then rehearse this out loud several times before actually shooting the video. Yes it needs to be OUT LOUD. Trust me. There is just something different about doing it out loud than thinking about it in your mind.

Of course if you are doing more of a power point video or webinar you will have slides to guide you the whole way so that makes it a lot easier.

Choose a custom thumbnail image

Did you know you can change the image that people see when are searching for videos? You can. And if you're not selecting the image or adding an amazing image you are losing out on views.

You can add a custom thumbnail in YouTube by going to your "video manager" then clicking "edit" – on the right side of the screen you will see 3 thumbnail options that YouTube has already provided for you – or you can click the button right underneath them that says "custom thumbnail" – this is the button you are looking for.

Now you need to create an image that is 1280x720 to upload as your thumbnail. If your already somewhat tech savvy all you need to do is take a screenshot of your youtube video – then add a caption over the top using a tool like picmonkey.com

If you're not so tech savvy you might need some more help so here is YouTube video to walk you through the process step-by-step:

https://youtu.be/tnz_yuK9qoM

Add Music

Depending on the type of video you are shooting adding background music or intro/outro music can make a big difference in the energy level of the video.

But don't go spending a fortune on background music. Here are a couple of sites you can get "royalty free" background music.

http://Pond5.com

http://PremiumBeat.com

Increase your energy level

Just like music can add energy to the video...so can you. Video really knocks down the energy level so make sure you watch the first cut of your video and make sure your

energy level is coming across how you would like it to.

Top 7 Video Distribution Sites

I mentioned earlier that that YouTube is the biggest player when it comes to video marketing but you are mission out on potentially thousands of visitors by neglecting some of the other video distribution sites. Here are some other platforms you should upload your videos to:

- Youtube.com
- MetaCafe.com
- Viddler.com
- DailyMotion.com
- Blip.tv
- Vimeo.com
- Screen.yahoo.com

Now if the thought of uploading your video to all of those sites individually, adding your description, keywords, etc…. sounds like a daunting task I have good news for you.

There is a service called http://TubeMogul.com that will distribute the videos for you.

Paid Video Platforms

Sometimes you want to have more of a classy look to a video than hosting it on Youtube. Or you want to have enhanced video analytics so you can see things like; how many people have watch your video, how far into the video the person watched, if there is a point where lots of people are dropping off,etc…

For that reason there are a couple of paid platforms I really like.

1. Viimeo.com – (There is a paid version as well) I really like this platform if you just want a classy looking video player for your page that is not too expensive.
2. Wistia.com – I like this platform for tracking and analytics. It is much more expensive than Vimeo however the features are very robust.
3. Amazon s3 – This is a really great hosting site that allows you to "pay as you go" depending on how much your videos get played.

3 Keys to Success with Video Marketing

There are some people who start with video marketing and achieve very high levels of success. While others fail miserably! I want to help you be in the group of people that achieve high levels of success so here are 3 things that successful video marketers focus on in creating winning video marketing campaigns.

Creating Value

When you go to youtube or any other video platform you are usually looking for something of value right? For example, you might want to know "how to do_____" – or "the best _____".

This is what other people are looking for as well….VALUE!

So to have a great video marketing campaign you need come up with valuable content you can share in videos.

A great way to brainstorm ideas is to simply think about the most asked questions you get in your business. So maybe make list of the top 10 things you get asked all the time...then create a separate video for each question. You've now created value to put into the marketplace which positions you as a leader in the marketplace!

That leads me to the next point...

Keyword Research

To get your video in front of the most people you need to know what keywords people are searching for.

There are a couple of ways I do keyword research for YouTube videos.

So let's walk though an example of each that you can take and apply to your market.

#1 – Directly on YouTube

Let's say you sell Nike shoes. You want to know what people are searching for on YouTube related to Nike Shoes. All you have do is...

- Go the search bar and type in "Nike" but don't hit enter just yet.
- You'll see a dropdown of words below the search box that pull up
- Those are the most searched keywords that start with the work "Nike"

nike

nike **commercial**
nike **football**
nike **academy**
nike **soccer**
nike **sb**
nike **basketball**
nike **soccer commercial**
nike **air mag**
nike **fuel band**
nike **roshe run**

This is going to give you a great idea on how name your video title so you can get the most traffic for your video. Just make sure you use the most common keywords in your title.

I would suggest repeating this process 5-10x keywords you think you audience might be searching for so you have a complete list.

#2 – Google Keyword Research Tool

This is a free tool that Google provides so you can get a more clear idea of how many searches are being performed on the keywords you have found.

You can access the keyword tool here: http://adwords.google.com/keywordplanner

You want to choose "get search volume" once you login.

Type in your keyword ideas and Google will begin to give you the estimated search volume of each keyword.

I like to look for keywords that have anywhere from 5,000-30,000 searches per month. But you have to decide what make it worth it for you. Keywords that get less than 5,000 searches per month will get a lot less traffic but are probably not as competitive of search terms. That means it will be easier for you (typically) to jump in front of the other videos. Keywords with more than 30,000 searches have a lot more capability to drive you traffic however they are generally very competitive meaning other people are always trying to beat you out for a piece of that traffic.

Now that you have your keywords you want to try and use them in 2 places:
- The title of your video
- In the description box

This is going to help your video be found much faster and get you a lot more traffic!

Consistency

If you're just looking to use video to help boost a sales presentation on your web page or develop videos to help train employees consistency is not as big of a worry.

However if you are looking to get more traffic to your website you need to post on a consistent schedule.

Posting 1 video and waiting for the flood of traffic to come in is not going to work.

I would suggest posting at least 1 video per week to all of the distribution channels we have talked about. Of course the frequency is totally up to you I have just found that once per week is great number to shoot for across a lot of business models.

Video Marketing Metrics
(What You Should Be Tracking)

You've dedicated time, energy and money into creating a great video marketing campaign; now it's time for you to take a step back and analyze how the videos are performing. Because each campaign is unique, different metrics act as the main performance indicators. In this chapter we'll discuss the metrics you'll find most valuable to your brand.

These metrics are important to everyone from the expert marketer to content creators, advertisers and the average business owner. A large number of diligent and empirically motivated marketers don't handle video analytics the same way they do web analytics and conversion metrics and this has a terrible effect on their marketing campaigns.

Let's dig into correcting that.

1. Followers

Every video hosting platform and social media outlet have some sort of "likes" or "followers" The reason I'm listing this first is because you're building your audience. A lot of times a sale or a lead doesn't happen on the first connection but over time. If you can gain someone as a follower on your YouTube channel or they: "like" your page – it's still a win.

Im running a video campaign right now on Facebook for a client...I started with a fresh page so 0 "likes". And I'm running a post engagement video ad. Even though I'm not directly advertising for "likes" I've had 696 new likes on the page in just 7 days! Those people have now become my audience to follow up with again and again.

2. Engagement metrics

Along with followers, -Shares, Likes, and Comments around your video are should also be tracked.

Don't be afraid to engage with the people that are commenting and sharing your videos either. If they are engaged that's a great sign your building rapport.

3. Click-Through Rate

Click through rate is how many people watch your video vs how many click click on your website (or take the action you ask them to in the video).

If you have a strong call to action you should also have a great click-through rate! One of the big reasons you do video for you business is to get your audience to take some sort of action. So keep a close eye on this one and try and improve it over time.

4. Completion rate

Want to know just how compelling your message is? Completion rates will give you a fairly accurate idea. In case you have no idea what completion rates are, this is the percentage of people who watch the video to the end. It's a good way to measure how engaged the user is with your videos. If you find the percentage high it means that the content has been well aligned with the targeted audience.

According to TubeMogul, a software platform for digital marketing, viewers remember brand messages at a higher rate when they watch the entire ad: additionally, brand awareness grows significantly when viewers watch the full ad. A crucial metric for any video campaign, the completion rate will let you know how engaged and captive your audience is.

BONUS: YouTube SEO for #1 Google Rankings (Checklist)

So ranking your video on the first page of YouTube is one thing but how about taking your traffic the next level and getting your YouTube video on page #1 of Google?

I get thousands and thousands of visitors per week ranking my videos on page #1 of Google. This is definitely a place you should be spending some time.

You may have heard Google SEO is hard to do....but being one of my valued readers I wanted to make it very easy for you. So I'm going to include my YouTube SEO checklist. This is everything I do step-by-step to rank my Personal Videos on page #1. Its actually a very predictable process....just follow the system and it works every time.

Overall Formula
1. Create video
2. Upload and optimize
3. Promote video
4 Rinse and repeat

Optimize Your Video
1. Upload video to YouTube
2. Optimize the Title, Description, Tags
       Title - Main Keyword [Any extra text]
       Description - http://mysite.com – {Call to action}

       2-4 paragraphs description with keyword sprinkled in +
       semantic keywords sprinkled in.

       Title to video again
       http://linktothevideo.com

       Tags - keyword phrase + 3-5 variations of keyword phrase

3. Add Call to Action with link to "offer" (Mask any affiliate links)
4. Add secondary "link to Video" on YouTube
5. Create Play List and Add related popular videos (Use exact key phrase to name playlist)

Promote the video
1. Social Sharing (Facebook, Twitter, Stumbleupon, etc..)
2. Embed (blog post / or website store)
3. Build backlinks (Manually or automated)
Manual links
       -Web 2.o/social site links
       -Social Bookmark links
       -Other social sharing sites
       -Wiki links

-.org links
Outsourced links (Use Fiverr.com - Only for backlinks to
YouTube video - not your personal website)
- 100% real youtube views
- .edu and .gov links
- Add site to 600 social bookmarks + rss + ping +
seo backlinks
- http://onehourbacklinks.co/
4. Get real youtube views if needed to boost the SEO even
more
-Virool.com (optional)

Conclusion

I really hope you have found value in this book. These are

exact steps I use to get thousands of views per month to

both my own videos and websites as well as for clients. If

you follow this outline I know you too can be successful

with video marketing! If I had one more piece of advice it

would be to just dig in! Even if it all seems overwhelming

just do it....everything is overwhelming until its not.

All the Best,

Chris King

P.S. Again I really hope you have found value in this book and have found some golden nuggets to use in your business. If you have I would really appreciate if you would leave a 5 start review on Amazon to let others know your experience.